Yohji Yamamoto

Translated from the French by Jane Brenton

First published in Great Britain in 1997
by Thames and Hudson Ltd, London

British Library Cataloguing-in-Publication Data
A catalogue record for this book is available from
the British Library

ISBN 0-500-01815-4

Printed and bound in Italy

Yohji Yamamoto

by François Baudot

Thames and Hudson

‘People wear my clothes to make a statement,’ explained Yohji Yamamoto, summing up, in the laconic style we have become familiar with over the last twenty or more years, a contribution to fashion that constitutes an exploration of fashion itself.

For his was not the leisured opulence of haute couture, the flashy brilliance of prêt-à-porter, nor even the futuristic vision of the avant-garde. What became clear, gradually but inexorably, as we followed the Japanese designer’s reespousal of the great archetypes of fashion, his choice of a neutral vocabulary, his adoption of a simplified palette and range, was the power and essential difference of the Yamamoto style. It was an approach which, while taking into account the contribution of Paris couture, and indeed traditional Japanese costume, nevertheless set out quite deliberately to tap new areas of creative potential in the domain of fashion in all its modes and manifestations – a world that had experienced more fresh starts in a single turbulent century than it had in the previous thousand years.

Throughout the 1950s, the couturiers had reigned supreme, but in the following decade they found themselves challenged by the growing success of the 'stylistes'. These stylists had more to do in the beginning with the promotion of the big industrial brandnames, but they became the focus of a generation that acquired the name 'jeunes créateurs' – a somewhat tautological description applied in this instance to a galaxy of talent essentially Paris-based, though later embracing a sprinkling of Italian imitators who in many cases benefited from the superior logistical back-up. Between 1965 and 1985, a whole variety of trends in prêt-à-porter flourished briefly, met their demise or prospered: these were instigated both by the big-name couturiers and by designers outside the charmed circle. It was an essentially centrifugal movement, bizarre and extravagant in its traditions, and its very success eventually caused it to lose momentum. In the early eighties, it was superseded by the new wave of so-called conceptualists. This term, taken from the plastic arts, referred back to the conceptual art of the sixties, whose practitioners sought to replace the work of art itself with the idea underlying it, the project of its gestation, the analysis of its concept and its effects. In other words, precisely the sort of 'statement' to which Yohji Yamamoto referred.

Although conceptual art has often been deemed elitist and inward-looking, in fact its practitioners were from the outset concerned to find common points of reference with their public. They did this by seeking inspiration in the real world. Today, ten years on – that being the minimum amount of time it requires – fashion is taking its cue from these artists (though with the difference that the original artists were not obliged to operate within the market economy). Even Marcel Duchamp is an influence, as, too, is the creative explosion represented by Minimalism – Ad Reinhardt's monochromes or the primary structures of Donald Judd, Sol LeWitt or Carl André – and also Arte Povera, with its accumulations, the assemblages of Jannis Kounellis, Mario Merz, Giulio Paolini.... These movements in contemporary art all represent an attempt to engage with everyday life. Whether by looking with fresh eyes at a pile of stones, a torn advertising poster, or neon signs in the city, the aim is the same: to find a way of prompting the imagination and setting it free.

although he would not go so far as to lay claim to the status of artist, in his approach to clothes Yohji Yamamoto shows himself to be exceptionally responsive to contemporary trends – in the same way that couturiers of preceding generations responded to Cubism, say, or the Ballets Russes or Pop Art. Caught up in the delirium of the seventies, was not Andy Warhol heard to remark, 'When you think about it, department stores are kind of like museums.' (Indeed he went so far as to reverse the formula, explaining that he liked Rome because it was a sort of museum, 'like Bloomingdale's'.) Arte Povera went further still, with its refusal to be seduced by smooth surfaces, Pop colours and the consumer society, opting instead for basic elements that had not been transmuted: wood shavings, rags, mud, coal, and so on. In the 'roaring eighties', Yohji Yamamoto would attempt something comparable – one of a small number who tried to break away from a fossilized conception of what clothes were. He did this by disrupting the codes by which clothes made their appeal; by rethinking the glamorous signals sent out by their external appearance; by redefining their relationship with the male or female body; and, ultimately – to near universal incomprehension – by radically reinterpreting the respective contributions of beauty and ugliness, past and future, memory and modernity.

In this revolutionary endeavour, a central role is played by the colour black, 'ultimate darkness and universal silhouette'. (Earlier this century, it had also been Chanel's secret weapon.) For Yamamoto's collections are veritable hymns to darkness, devoid of jewelry, decoration and detail, investing his silhouette with a sense of mystery. In a society that glorifies and exalts the body and exposes it to view, Yohji has invented a new code of modesty. This is fashion that recognizes no boundaries; it is ageless and timeless, with clothes stripped of all affectation, reduced to their essentials: to an argument for a dress, a proposal for a jacket, an abstract idea of a woman. Faced with the irreversible decline of the traditional values of elegance, Yamamoto transposes them to an aesthetic and technological environment that is resolutely contemporary. Exploring the history of clothing in all its most ascetic variations, the Yamamoto style celebrates and at the same time incessantly questions the ambiguous marriage between the enduring and the ephemeral. Out of this, as at all great moments in fashion, 'classics' are born – contemporary forms imbued with a wealth of historical references that secretly perpetuate themselves in new guises.

Yohji Yamamoto – his name means 'at the mountain's foot' – was born in Tokyo in 1943. A child of the Japanese defeat, haunted by the sight of the ruins on which Japan was rebuilding its future, his only support came from his mother, a war widow, who worked sixteen hours a day as a dressmaker. The first 'woman in black' in his life, she dreamed he would become a lawyer and sent him to university. With little enthusiasm, he tried to mingle with the Japanese elite, adopt its codes and programmed objectives. To his mother's consternation, he finally decided to go back and work in her shop. She imposed one condition, that he should attend the famous Bunka School of Fashion to acquire a basic knowledge of his craft. Those were difficult years for Yamamoto, full of humiliations and resentments. Quite apart from the fact that he was the only boy, he was also the oldest pupil there. And all that his mother's customers wanted from him were slavish copies of the latest Parisian models. Happily, the small amount of money he earned enabled him to make up designs of his own.

In 1969, Yamamoto won a competition offering a trip to Paris as the first prize. With not a sou to his name, he survived eight months in the world's fashion capital. It was long enough to discover the existence of the job of 'styliste'. He spoke not one single word of French. He ate practically nothing but observed everything: especially the prêt-à-porter that flourished in those days around Saint-Germain-des-Prés. Here was a life that appealed to him. Back in Tokyo in 1972, he founded the 'Y's Company Ltd', his first fashion business, which showed its opening collection in 1977. By 1981, he was in Paris, where his show had its audience literally rooted to the spot. That was the year in which not only Yohji Yamamoto's collection but also the collection designed by Rei Kawakubo, his former companion, would force the representatives of the world's press to examine their consciences: ought they to countenance the possibility of a change in the well-oiled system of fashion and the collections? In the audience, knowing laughter of the most reactionary sort was punctuated with gasps of horror. Yet just a few days later, the two unknowns were famous.

The day after the collections, *Libération* carried a headline: 'French fashion has found its masters: the Japanese.' Beneath it appeared the following prophetic words, written by Michel Cressole: 'The outfits he offers us in 1982 for us to wear in the next twenty years are infinitely more feasible than those proposed by Courrèges and Cardin in around 1960 for the year 2000, which today look as old hat as a Soviet sci-fi film. French couturiers have for too long clung to the view that couture, like science, was the rectification of a long period of error. The Japanese stylists, on the other hand, prepare ... the women of the planet Earth for being able to decide in an instant what clothes and accessories to take with them when they have only half an hour to make their escape.'

A businessman as much as a creative talent – even if he once insisted he was not interested in money, and had very little anyway – Yohji Yamamoto, fifteen years after that prediction, finds himself at the head of eight companies. Now it is his mother who works for him.

It was in 1984 that he launched his attack on that other bastion of conservatism, the man's suit. To create a fitting companion for woman-according-to-Yohji, the three-piece suit with its associations of stuffy formality would have to go. It was replaced by prototypical garments that were fluid and disciplined masterpieces of understatement. White shirts with a severity untainted by authoritarianism, embodying the architecture of a new classicism. Narrow lapels, narrow shoulders, three-button jacket, trousers tight to the knee and resting on a well-polished black shoe. For more than ten years now, the trend has been irreversible, this has been 'the look' for men. Yet it is all achieved with a deftness of touch and a timelessness that is reassuring for the many men who hate to feel they are fashion victims. In a recent film set in Germany between the wars, the costume designer simply dressed the actors in Yamamoto. No one noticed anything out of place, no hint of 'retro'.

'If fashion is clothes, then it is not indispensable. But if fashion is a way of looking at our daily lives, then it is very important indeed. Of the so-called arts – painting, sculpture, etc. – only very few can influence people directly in the way fashion can, or music. Fashion is a unique and fundamental form of communication, that has to do with the feelings of a generation wearing the clothes it has chosen.' Yamamoto is the most philosophical and the wisest of fashion designers – perhaps also the one who often appears the most disillusioned.

'Making a garment means thinking about people. I am always eager to meet people and talk to them. It's what I like more than anything else. What are they doing? What are they thinking? How do they lead their lives? And then I can set to work. I start with the fabric, the actual material, the "feel" of it. I then move on to the form. Possibly what counts most for me is the feel. And then, when I start working on the material, I think my way into the form it ought to assume.' The construction of all of Yohji Yamamoto's garments starts from the two points just above the shoulder blades. From there the cloth hangs best, allowing the material to take on a life of its own.

When the first Yamamoto model insinuated itself into the brilliant, structured, over-accessorized world of Paris prêt-à-porter in the eighties, the line was loose-fitting. The garment stood right away from the body it delicately encased, apparently never touching it. Usually thick, opaque and dark in colour, it often seemed to be standing up by itself. Of positively medieval severity, it had a second-hand look about it that prompted some to describe it as post-punk (grunge was still light years away). It looked lived-in, as though it had acquired a patina with the passage of time, like those items in our wardrobe that have become special favourites. It reflected that hatred of what is new that is so wonderfully exemplified by a certain sort of English dandy who used to have his boots broken in for him and get his valet to wear his camel-hair suits for the first couple of years. To Wim Wenders, who made a feature film about him, the designer confided: 'My dream is to draw time.' One thinks of all those oversized capes, unstructured coats, asymmetric jackets. 'Symmetry – the symbol of perfection – is not sufficiently human.' And it is, precisely, to humanity that this master of scissors and fabric looks for his inspiration – to the work clothes worn by hundreds of anonymous figures; for example, those men and women from the German heartland who posed for the photographer August Sander between the wars. To boilersuits, dungarees, overalls, pea jackets. Even the railwayman's outfit made up of layers – the apotheosis of the tramp who carries his world on his back. A garment that becomes one with the person who wears it, so much a part of him that it is entirely subordinated to the force of his personality. 'Whether a season's fashion is interesting or not does not depend on the designers who created it, but on those who see it and buy it.'

And what of Japan in all this? Yohji Yamamoto, as a citizen of the world, recognizes his debt to the history of fashion and, in particular, the whole archaeology of couture. But he refuses to identify himself in terms of his Far Eastern origins. 'The Japanese influence? It simply doesn't interest me.' One of that country's greatest assets, he does not hold back on his criticisms of a system which, he admits, sometimes weighs heavily upon him.

'I happen to have been born in Japan. But I've never labelled myself in that way.' Yet it is difficult not to see in the subtle loops of cloth with which Yamamoto drapes his bodies, in the timelessness of his creations, and in the modesty and restraint of his mannequins, the effects of a particular tradition. The same mystery and silence, the same quality of abstraction, inhabit the silk of Japanese kimonos and Yamamoto's woollen yarns and synthetics... And then there is that extraordinary tension that occurs in the Far East – and that we in the rest of the world find so fascinating – between the simple and the sophisticated, between natural materials and technological advance, between the empire of the senses and the tempered discretion of the feelings. It is these same very particular paradoxes that are expressed, without anecdotal elaboration, in Yamamoto's person and in his work as an authentic couturier of everyday life. He is one of those few designers who have helped bring about a lasting transformation in the appearance of the men and women of the latter years of our century, by expressing their uncertainties, their fears and their contradictions, the passions of an age. And there is also a certain dignity – a virtue somewhat neglected in the last thirty years, but one which could turn out to have a future.

221
CAFE
ENTER

NEW YORK

RANZLER

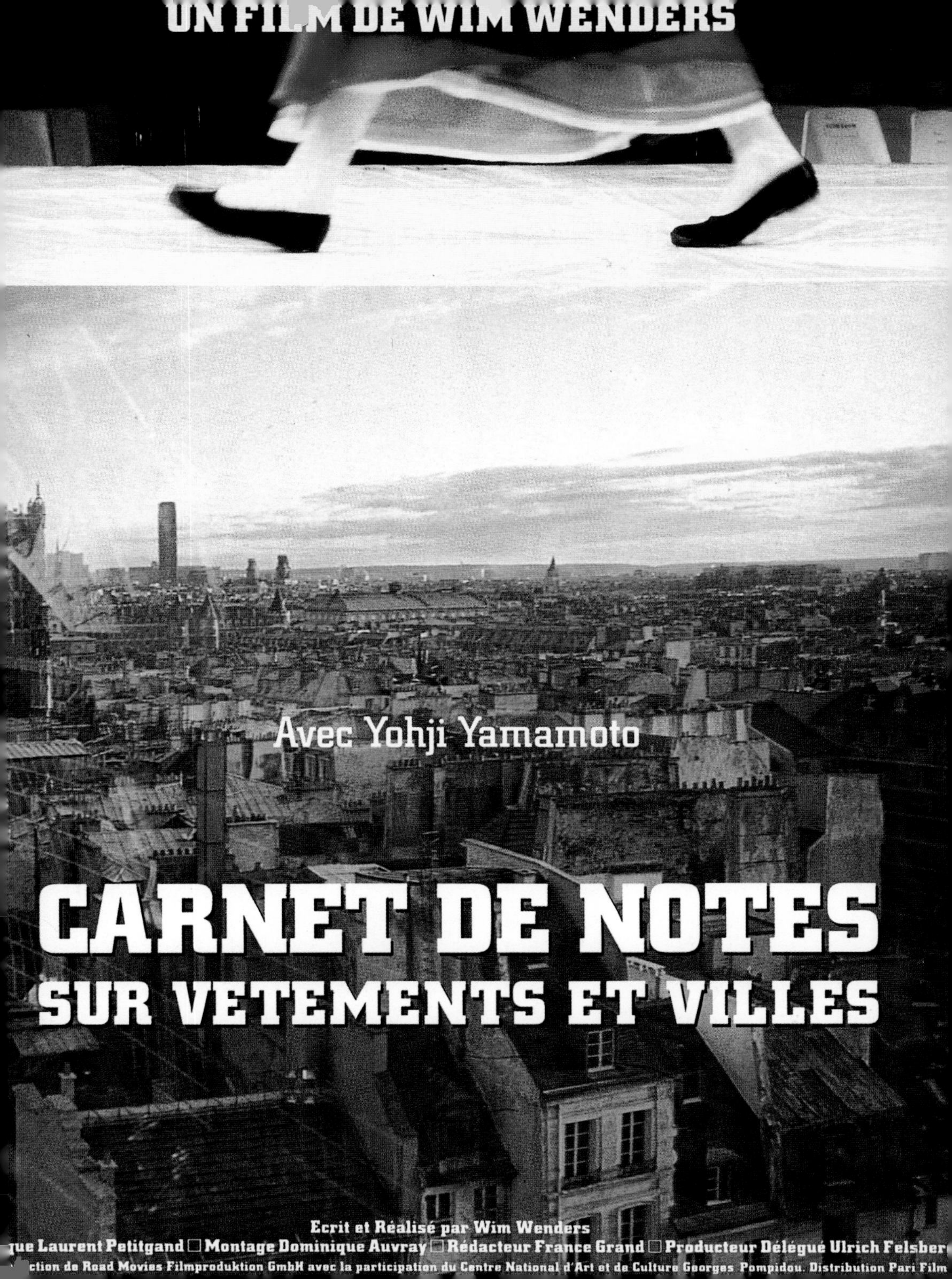
UN FILM DE WIM WENDERS
Avec Yohji Yamamoto
CARNET DE NOTES
SUR VETEMENTS ET VILLES
Ecrit et Réalisé par Wim Wenders
que Laurent Petitgand □ Montage Dominique Auvray □ Rédacteur France Grand □ Producteur Délégué Ulrich Felsber
ction de Road Movies Filmproduktion GmbH avec la participation du Centre National d'Art et de Culture Georges Pompidou. Distribution Pari Film

Chronology

1943 Birth of Yohji Yamamoto in Tokyo. His mother, Fumi Yamamoto, is a war widow. She works sixteen hours a day as a dressmaker to pay for her son's upbringing and education.

1966 Yohji studies Law at the University of Keio and is awarded his final diploma.

1969 Graduates from the famous Japanese fashion school Bunka Fukuso Gakuin.

1971 Opens his first business, the 'Y's Company Ltd'.

1977 Having for some years produced several collections each season, he decides to adopt the practice of other leading Japanese designers and show with them in Tokyo.

1981 The decisive moment of his career comes when his work is seen in Paris, as part of the week of fashion shows devoted to the prét-à-porter collections of couturiers and fashion designers. He also shows in New York.

1982 Yohji Yamamoto is awarded the twenty-sixth Fashion Editors Club Award in Tokyo.

1984 First 'Yamamoto pour Homme' collection.

1989 The Centre de Création Industrielle of the Musée d'Art Moderne at the Centre Georges Pompidou commissions the director Wim Wenders to make a film about Yohji Yamamoto. The resulting feature-length film is shot in 35mm, in colour, and is entitled *Carnets de notes sur vêtements et villes* (*Notebook on cities and clothes*).

1990 Yohji Yamamoto is commissioned to design the costumes for Puccini's *Madam Butterfly* in a production by the Opéra de Lyon. The set designs are by Avatalsozaki.

1991 Yohji Yamamoto is awarded the thirty-fifth Fashion Editors Club Award in Tokyo.

1993 The Bayreuth Festival commissions Yamamoto to design the costumes for Wagner's *Tristan and Isolde* in a production by Heiner Müller with Daniel Barenboim as musical director.

1994 The French Ministry of Culture appoints Yamamoto a Chevalier de l'Ordre des Arts et des Lettres.

1995 Pina Baush, Fanny Ardant, Jean Nouvel, Juliette Binoche, Sandrine Kimberlain, Wim Wenders and Karl Lagerfeld are among those seen wearing Yohji Yamamoto's clothes. Launch of the new 'Plus Noir' collection for women, urban and classical in mood.

1996 Launch of 'Yohji', the designer's first perfume, created and manufactured in France by Jean Patou.

Silhouettes in the fog. Autumn/Winter 1985–86. Photo: Jean-François Deroubaix.

Yamamoto

Long reversible coat in rust-yellow wool and black net. Catalogue Yohji Yamamoto, Autumn/Winter 1995–96. © David Sims.
Loose coat with crushed effect. Catalogue Yohji Yamamoto, Autumn/Winter 1984–85. © Max Vadakul.

New York. Catalogue Yohji Yamamoto, Autumn/Winter 1984–85. © Max Vadukul.

Asymmetric ribbed jersey with extra-long sleeves. Catalogue Yohji Yamamoto, Autumn/Winter 1992–93. Photo: Dominique Isserman. © *Vogue* France.
Catalogue Yohji Yamamoto. Spring/Summer 1985. © Max Vadukul.

Long dress with loose-fitting sleeves in a jungle print. Catalogue Yohji Yamamoto, Spring/Summer 1985. © Max Vadakul.
Suit in loosely woven black and white silk tweed. Catalogue Yohji Yamamoto, Spring/Summer 1997. © Paolo Roversi.

Suit in white silk chiffon. Catalogue Yohji Yamamoto, Spring/Summer 1997. Photo: Peter Lindbergh for *Vogue* Italy © Peter Lindbergh.
Catalogue Yohji Yamamoto. Autumn/Winter 1986–87.© Nick Knight.

A fitting in progress in Yohji Yamamoto's workroom in Tokyo. ©Jeremy Stigler.

The twice-weekly fitting in the atelier. With his assistants standing by, Yohji Yamamoto puts the finishing touches to the models in his collection. Here, the object of intense scrutiny is a suit in the Autumn/Winter 1993–94 collection. Photo: Jean-Marie Perier for *Elle*. © *Elle* Scoop.

Yohji Yamamoto in Paris, making final revisions to the order of the show for the collection of Spring/Summer 1991. Photo: Thierry Bouët. © *Marie-Claire* Germany.

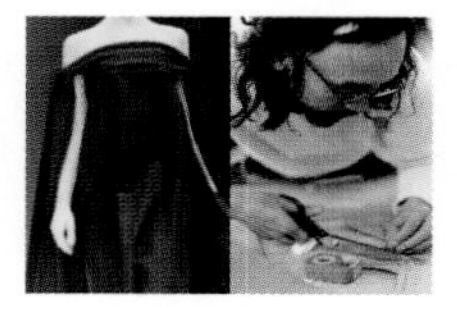

Evening gown in black gabardine, with effect of knotted scarf around the bust. Spring/Summer 1993. © Yutaka Yamamoto.
The master of cutting calculates to the millimetre rather than the centimetre: Yohji Yamamoto never hesitates to intervene personally in the production of a prototype. © Yutaka Yamamoto.

Long jacket with 'magpie' tail, from the 'Tango' collection. Catalogue Yohji Yamamoto, Autumn/Winter 1985–86. © Paolo Roversi.
Draped coat in red wool velvet. Catalogue Yohji Yamamoto, Autumn/Winter 1987–88. © Nick Knight.

Long coat in carded red wool covered with a fine nylon mesh. Catalogue Yohji Yamamoto, Autumn/Winter 1995–96. © David Sims.
'Kimono' coat dress. Spring/Summer 1995. Illustration: François Berthoud. © Galerie Bartsch et Chariau.

Black wool gabardine ensemble. Autumn/Winter 1995–96. Photo: Nathaniel Goldberg. © Donna.
Catalogue Yohji Yamamoto. Autumn/Winter 1987–88. © Nick Knight.

Coat in black woollen cloth with mottled weave. Catalogue Yohji Yamamoto, Autumn/Winter 1995–96. © David Sims.
Stole in olive-green woollen cloth. Catalogue Yohji Yamamoto, Autumn/Winter 1988–89. © Nick Knight.

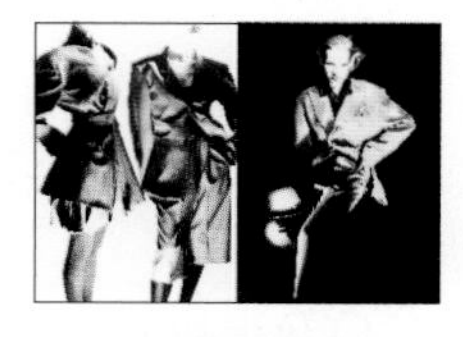

Catalogue Yohji Yamamoto. Autumn/Winter 1987–88. © Nick Knight.
Jacket in light brown rayon with decorative buttons, Catalogue Yohji Yamamoto, Spring/Summer 1988. © Nick Knight.

Asymmetric jacket in navy wool gabardine over a white satin skirt. Catalogue Yohji Yamamoto, Autumn/Winter 1987–88. © Nick Knight.

Shadow play of Japanese silhouettes. Catalogue Yohji Yamamoto, Autumn/Winter 1987–88. © Nick Knight.

Fitted jacket over a long dress and skirt in wool cloth edged with fur, 'Poupées Russes' collection, Autumn/Winter 1990–91. Photo: Peter Lindbergh for *Vogue* Italy. © Condé Nast Publications, SPA.

Long frock coat in maroon wool cloth over a skirt in black wool cloth. Catalogue Yohji Yamamoto, Autumn/Winter 1988–89. © Nick Knight.
Bra-dress and wide-brimmed hat in yellow silk satin. Catalogue Yohji Yamamoto, Spring/Summer 1997. © Paolo Reversi.

Long dress in tricot and black wool gabardine with leaf prints made by the traditional Japanese technique of 'yusen'. Autumn/Winter 1995–96. © *Marie-Claire*.
Poster for the film *Carnet de notes sur vêtements et villes* (*Notebook on cities and clothes*), written and directed by Wim Wenders in 1989, commissioned by the CCI, Centre Georges Pompidou. © Archives Yohji Yamamoto.

White cotton shirt worn over a long black skirt. Spring/Summer 1985. Photo: Eddy Kohll. © *Marie-Claire Bis*.
Draped wrap-around jacket in red wool cloth over a long black woollen skirt. Autumn/Winter 1985–86. Photo: Eddy Kohll. Courtesy of *Harper's and Queen*. © The National Magazine Company.

Effect of scarlet and black. Long sheath dresses with full-length sleeves and red tulle bustles. On the catwalk at the Autumn/Winter 1986/87 collection. © Paolo Roversi.
Back to the classics with this black gabardine suit worn over a white cotton shirt. Catalogue Yohji Yamamoto, Spring/Summer 1997. © Paolo Roversi.

Reversible frock coat in two colours. Autumn/Winter 1993–94. Photo: Catalina Cot. © Glamour France.
Detail of the preceding model, worn here over a black leather waistcoat. Autumn/Winter 1993–94. © Alfredo Albertone.

Jacket with fitted waist and kimono sleeves in black wool with mottled weave worn over a long black taffeta skirt. Autumn/Winter 1995–96 collection. © Alfredo Albertone.
Knitted coat with mottled effect. Autumn/Winter 1996–97. Photo: Paolo Roversi for *Vogue* Italy. © Paolo Roversi.

Double-breasted coat dress in black silk satin over a bra-dress in yellow silk satin. Spring/Summer 1997. Photo: Sarah Moon. © *Elle* Scoop.
Unstructured evening dress in black silk satin. Catalogue Yohji Yamamoto, Spring/Summer 1997. © Paolo Roversi.

Black leather cape. Autumn/Winter 1988–89. © Nick Knight.
Stole in olive-green wool cloth, Autumn/Winter 1988–89. Photo: Arthur Elgort for *Vogue* France. © Arthur Elgort.

Fine-weave woollen dress knotted at the thigh. Catalogue Yohji Yamamoto, Spring/Summer 1988. © Nick Knight.
White wide-brimmed hat in the shape of a flower, with cut-outs. Catalogue Yohji Yamamoto, Spring/Summer 1988. © Nick Knight.

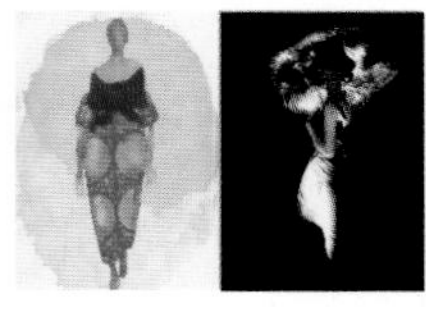

Kimono dress in black tricot and orange and gold brocade. Catalogue Yohji Yamamoto, Spring/Summer 1995. Illustration: Mats Gustafson. © Mats Gustafson.
Wrap-around pinafore dress. Spring/Summer 1988. © Nick Knight.

Sketch by Yohji Yamamoto for the 'Poupées Russes' collection, Autumn/Winter 1990–91. © Yohji Yamamoto.
Fitted jacket with basque over long reversible wool skirt. Autumn/Winter 1997–98 collection. © Alfredo Albertone.

Yohji with his mother, Fumi Yamamoto, and his guitar. The former gave him not only life but also his first opportunity to show his talents as a designer. The latter is the means by which he expresses his aspirations towards a better world. Photo: Françoise Huguier. © *Marie-Claire*.

The publishers wish to thank the house of Yamamoto for its assistance in producing this book, and especially Irène Silvagni, Nathalie Ours and Laurence.

We are also greatly indebted to Nick Knight, and to David Sims, Sarah Moon, Max Vadukul, Dominique Issermann and Paolo Roversi.

Finally, this book would not have been possible without the help and co-operation of various agencies. Our thanks go to: Emma Wheeler (Nick Knight), Barry Rock (David Sims), Vincent Simonet (Marion de Beaupré), Alexandra (Dominique Issermann), Arnaud (Outline), Sandrine (Michele Filomeno), Michelle (Arthur Elgort Ltd) Joëlle Chariau (Galerie Bartsch et Chariau) and Rosanna Sguera (Art & Commerce).